I0037437

How to be a Good Manager and Supervisor, and How to Delegate

Lessons Learned from the Trenches: Insider Secrets for Managers and Supervisors

Richard G Lowe, Jr

How to be a Good Manager and Supervisor, and How to Delegate

Lessons Learned from the Trenches: Insider Secrets for Managers and Supervisors

Business Professional Series #2

Published by The Writing King
www.thewritingking.com

How to be a Good Manager and Supervisor, and How to Delegate

Copyright © 2016 by Richard G Lowe, Jr.

All rights reserved. No part of this publication may be reproduced, stored in a retrieval system, or transmitted by any means – electronic, mechanical, photographic (photocopying), recording, or otherwise – without prior permission in writing from the author.

Although every precaution has been taken to verify the accuracy of the information contained herein, the author and publisher assume no responsibility for any errors or omissions. No liability is assumed for damages that may result from the use of information contained within.

Trademarked names appear throughout this book. Rather than use a trademark symbol with every occurrence of a trademarked name, names are used in an editorial fashion, with no intention of infringement of the respective owner's trademark.

Cover Artist: theamateurzone

ASIN: B016R7M91W
ISBN: 978-1-943517-71-8 (Hardcover)
ISBN: 978-1-943517-70-1 (Paperback)
ISBN: 978-1-943517-14-5 (eBook)

Audiobook narrated by Robin McKay

Table of Contents

Introduction

"A manager is not a person who can do the work better than his men; he is a person who can get his men to do the work better than he can." —Frederick W. Smith

What if I told you that most of what school teaches about supervising and managing people is misguided, wrong, and will make your job more challenging? Would you be shocked, or would you nod your head knowingly because that's something that you have felt for a long time but were afraid to speak out loud?

Working for a good manager can be an incredibly fulfilling experience because they understand how to delegate authority, responsibility, and tasks to individuals and groups. Poor managers assign tasks, arbitrarily set deadlines, and then, to add insult to injury, don't provide adequate resources to achieve the goals. To meet unrealistically assigned objectives, team members have to work long hours, often without additional compensation (salaried workers generally do not receive overtime pay.)

The truly outstanding manager empowers people to work individually and as a group to work towards the common good of everyone involved. Deadlines are set after consultation with the team, the required resources are assigned, and authority and responsibility are delegated appropriately.

There are plenty of management books out there, and I'm not even going to attempt to write yet another tome explaining a

Introduction

fad management technique. That's not the purpose of this book.

My goal is to impart to you – my reader – a philosophy of how to succeed as a manager or supervisor of people. You can attend college to learn techniques of how to robotically manage a group. Lots of people in the workplace do exactly that, and many of them become good managers. However, the best learning comes from mentors, short courses, books and from the school of hard knocks—experience.

Way back in 1981, I was hired out of college by a teacher who decided he wanted to start a company of his own. He had been working for Digital Equipment Corporation—a company that later merged with Compaq, which then merged with Hewlett-Packard—supporting customers all over the Southern California area. He formed a rapport with these clients and decided that he could do a better job delivering services via his own company.

I was their first employee, and my experience consisted of three computer classes. The big advantage for my teacher was that I was cheap, I could produce quality code quickly, and I had a lot of promise.

This job was an excellent break for me, and it was great for them because they gained a good employee whom they could mold into what they needed for a rather unique position.

Within a couple of years, I was promoted into a supervisory role. The company was tiny, and while everyone had vast technical experience, none of us had any supervisory or management experience. Managing groups of people was just as new to my managers as it was to me. We proceeded on this intimidating journey together, learning the ropes from a few successes, a few failures, and many hard learning experiences.

I wrote this book because many technical people get promoted into supervisory or management positions in the same way that I did. One day they are a programmer, a writer, a designer, or an assembly line worker, and the next they find themselves in charge of people. Often there is no preparation, no formal schooling, no training, and not even a mentor to help them along.

When I was initially promoted to a supervisory position, it felt incredible that I was entrusted with so much responsibility. I soon learned that supervising people, and later managing an entire department, was a lot more challenging than I would've thought. At the time, I had no formal classes in business or management and no training in supervising at all. I was a programmer, a coder, and, to make it even more challenging, a bit of an introvert. The learning curve was huge, and I made a few errors along the way, but in spite of all that I became a good leader and a good manager.

Motivating other people to get tasks done can be very fulfilling. On the other hand, being "the boss" can be a challenging and often demoralizing role.

Introduction

People that you supervise can be a fickle and finicky group, especially if you didn't hire them in the first place. Whether they mention it to you or not, they will judge you constantly, silently watching how you treat others, how your boss treats you, and how you relate to your peers. The example that you set and the image that you portray can mean the difference between success, barely keeping your head above water and failure. Like children, employees will constantly test your boundaries, and you need to enforce the limits fairly and occasionally ruthlessly.

Your peers, those individuals on the same level of the organizational chart as you, are vital to your success. You have to manage these people almost as much as those you supervise. Of course, you can't order them around or dictate to them, but most likely you need the services that their groups provide and their support to run your own team.

Your boss often has demands that he won't or can't explain, but he has to pass on to you. He may be under tremendous pressure and stress, which he can't or won't tell you about, but whether he wants to or not, you're going to feel it also.

Worst of all, there will be people above your boss on the organization chart who come to you with things they need to get done and demands they need to be fulfilled. While these requests are often well-meaning, they make an end run around your boss that may result in work that has nothing to do with your job.

As a boss, you need to follow company procedures and policies even if you don't agree with them. In fact, there will be occasions when you find yourself defending rules that you know are idiotic or wrong. That's just part of being a boss; you have to support the organization regardless of your personal feelings.

This book is intended to be a series of tips and techniques which I've learned over the years. These have brought me to terms with being the boss, taught me to play the role of manager and supervisor, and helped me succeed for over 35 years.

I hope you enjoy what I've written and find it to be of some value. If you would like to send me a note about this book, feel free to write me at rich@thewritingking.com. If you enjoyed the book, please write a positive review.

Suddenly Promoted

After working at Software Techniques, a small computer consulting company based in Southern California, for about a year I was suddenly promoted to a supervisory position. Before that, my role was applications programmer and technical writer, with a little bit of design and analysis thrown into the mix.

At that point in my life, I had absolutely no experience in management or supervision. I hadn't taken any courses on the subject, and to make it even worse, I was very introverted and shy.

Needless to say, it was a rough transition for me, although I didn't recognize it at the time. Being the boss was a whole new realm, and I did a pretty good job considering the situation.

My first undertaking – literally on the first day after being promoted – I fired another employee. In hindsight, that was a pretty bold move on my part. The employee needed to be terminated, as he had a gift for upsetting our clients, but still, letting someone go on my first day?

Within two weeks, I did my first hire—a programmer. She was a decent coder, but she had a drinking problem that reduced her afternoon productivity immensely and made her belligerent in the workplace. Before long, I was in the midst justifying her termination, but she made it easy by quitting.

Suddenly Promoted

Like many small companies, we had cash flow problems that created crippling situations with my teammates. The company never missed a payroll, but I remember the feelings of shock and betrayal when a couple of paychecks bounced. Money was found and the people got paid, but I found myself in the position—since I was the boss—of having to defend the indefensible.

At the same time, since we were a consulting company, one of my roles was to get new customers and managing existing clients. This was also new to me, and I found sales to be even more challenging than supervising people.

I assigned one of my subordinates, Silvester, to work at a client site. About four months later the client terminated the contract and we lost the business. Six months after that, the client hired Silvester to complete the work that we had been contracted to perform. After a painful conversation with the owner of that business, I found out that Silvester had made a deal to take over the contract himself personally after we were thrown out. That was when we realized that we need to include non-compete clauses in our employee contracts.

"Those people who develop the ability to continuously acquire new and better forms of knowledge that they can apply to their work and to their lives will be the movers and shakers in our society for the indefinite future." —Brian Tracy

I attended many classes to become a better manager. Continuing education, in my opinion, is essential to success in the workplace, and I've found it to be far more valuable than college. This is because continuation courses tend to be short and highly focused on the information needed to produce results. College is necessary for a general education, but continuing education can fill in the gaps and produce astonishing results quickly.

As time went by, I gained more experience at supervising my team. Those first few years were very challenging, and it wasn't just because I was green as a manager; the owners of the company and senior management were also new to this whole game.

The entire group consisted of people in their lower- to mid-20s, and while everyone was very experienced at their technical roles, management and supervision was brand new.

One of the lessons that I learned during that six-year period was the importance of recognizing your actual knowledge level, capability, and skill set. Managers higher than me on the organization chart often seemed to have difficulty understanding that they were just as new to all of this is I was.

Like many young people, every single one of us—myself included—suffered from arrogance and had an unwillingness to admit that we could be wrong about anything. We also had little, if any, desire to reach out for outside help. This was probably a result of having no money to spare combined with a bit of arrogance.

There is no place in the workplace for arrogance. A boss is not better than the people he or she supervises. They just have a fancy title, may have more experience and training, and usually make more money. This is true regardless of

Suddenly Promoted

whether they are the CEO of a multibillion-dollar, multinational company or just one of two people in a small startup.

One of the most demeaning moments of working for that first company was when a subordinate was promoted over me to become my boss. This situation produced enormous tension which could be felt in the air. To make matters worse, I had given him two solid years of bad reviews and poor raises. In spite of that, n my managers felt the need to promote him over me.

As it turned out, he actually was a decent manager who did right by me, but it was a difficult situation. In spite of the awkwardness, both of us adjusted, but that job was never the same for me again.

The lesson I learned from that situation was sometimes the game can be changed by external forces in ways that you can't predict. You have to adjust, learn the ropes, deal with any emotions that are stirred up, and get on with doing your job.

A big lesson from this time period was that it's important to keep your options open at all times. I realized that my managers could easily have chosen to let me go, or my new boss could have made my life miserable to get me to leave on my own. From this point forward, I made sure that my resume was always up-to-date, and I built up enough savings in the bank to survive for at least six months if the worst happened.

In hindsight, the great thing about working for that tiny little startup for six years was the amount of learning and experience that I gained. My office was just a few steps from the CEO of the company, and I was involved in many of the decisions that were made. I learned how to be fast and nimble, how to make decisions quickly, and I got to see how things operated at all levels of the organization chart.

Much of that is invisible when you're working in a larger company. The CEO may be in a separate building or even a different city. The HR and accounting departments are probably nowhere near you. The reasons behind how everything works may not be visible at all.

Since I was at that job from the very beginning – being its first employee – I had the opportunity to hire many different people. My team eventually consisted of six individuals who reported directly to me. Turnover was almost nonexistent until the company laid off one-third of its staff due to low sales. During the entire time I was there, three people left on their own, and three others got pushed out the door. The environment was safe, the camaraderie was good, and the morale was generally high.

A pleasant working environment, a feeling of camaraderie, and high morale will make up for a lot of negatives.

A manager, first of all, must ensure that the goals of the group that she supervises are in alignment with the objectives of the organization. Everyone on the team needs to be going in the same direction, and anything that is not in alignment needs to be discarded. After that, a manager must ensure sure that his or her team has a safe environment, that everyone works well together, and that they feel good about the place where they work.

Suddenly Promoted

A good foundation is laid by hiring people who fit the culture of the business rather than trying to fulfill some formula of education, skills, and experience. While those things are important, finding individuals who fit into the company culture is a much better way to ensure success.

Thus, a manager's job begins by hiring the right people. Quality individuals who fit the culture will make the job easier. Hiring new staff who don't believe in or fit into the environment of the company is going to make the entire team miserable and make your job harder.

Hiring

"We focus on two things when hiring. First, find the best people you can in the world. And second, let them do their work. Just get out of their way." —Matt Mullenweg

I personally hired over 100 people in the course of my 35-year career beginning as an application coder and ending as the Director of the computer operations department of a multi-billion dollar company. I've also observed over a thousand people and 100 managers go through the hiring process during that time span. In spite of classes, books, schooling, and mentoring, finding and hiring a person qualified for a position, and more importantly, a fit for the company culture, is a crapshoot at best. Hiring the wrong person can be a disaster.

Hiring can be one of the most agonizing things—next to firing—that any manager does. The whole process is filled with so much importance, at least on the surface, that it can be beyond stressful. In fact, making a wrong hiring decision be seen as a major failure that can haunt a manager's career for years.

Unfortunately, it is all but impossible to know how well a person will work out until she is actually on the job – producing – and has been doing so for at least six months. There are some techniques you can use to try and improve the odds of choosing the right person for the position, but it's just a matter of luck. This is especially true if you use the traditional methods of hiring using resumes or agents, also known as headhunters, to find people.

Hiring

There are many times when a candidate has had the perfect resume, interviewed exceptionally well, had excellent references that all checked out, and then turned out to be a babbling idiot on the job. This is true in all directions on the organization chart—up, down, and sideways.

On the other hand, some of the best people on my teams didn't have a resume, came dressed to the interview in casual clothes, and didn't provide any references.

Even so, a manager is expected to make a perfect hiring decision based on reading a resume, performing 1 to 3 interviews, and making a few phone calls to references.

Talk to your average manager and they will tell you that they have the process of hiring mastered. You'll hear how they start with the job description, skim resumes to discard those who are unqualified for the position, interview people, call references, and then make a hiring decision.

Let's look at this process in more detail. Typically, the procedure begins by placing an advertisement on various job hunting sites, engaging a couple of headhunters, and perhaps reaching out to a few fellow managers in other companies. Typically, dozens or even hundreds of resumes will be received for any position.

There had been times when I've advertised for a technical position and received anywhere from 500 to 1,000 resumes in a period of a single week. Of course, it is impossible to review or even quickly scan over that many resumes. To reduce this to a manageable level, some companies resort to keyword matching services to reject resumes that that don't show specific skills, experiences, or educational levels.

Ideally, a resume is a summary of a person's experience, skills, and education. The funny thing is, none of that has much to do with whether or not a person will work out. Obviously, a person's skills and knowledge are significant, but not vital. A person can always be trained and mentored to learn new things.

The most important question to answer when considering bringing someone on the team is, "Are they a good fit for the culture, company, and team members?" None of those things are mentioned on the resume, so why is the resume given so much importance in the hiring process?

The interview is supposed to fill the gap between the dry facts on the resume and the actual person, their capabilities, and personality. According to the theory, a manager should, in the course of less than an hour, talk to a person face-to-face and make a conclusion as to whether that person is the ideal candidate for the job. Some managers use phone interviews to screen out more candidates before taking the time to do them in person.

Quite a few managers don't bother to call references. Sometimes the human resources department performs reference checks, but these tend to be of questionable value. A few managers—very few—actually reach out to references, have real conversations with them, and find out useful information.

Hiring

Unfortunately, in today's litigious world, if you say something that causes someone not to get a job, you and your company can be sued. Thus, reference calls are often exercises in futility. You have to read between the lines and grasp at nonverbal cues to fill in the information that the person you're talking to can't tell you for fear of a lawsuit.

This is how modern businesses in the United States hire most of the time. They put out advertisements, receive a pile of resumes, filter out the junk, interview the rest, call some references, and make a decision. Sometimes I wonder if rolling dice or flipping a coin would make more sense.

This whole process for finding and hiring a person is, to be frank, unworkable, and it tends to find low-quality people.

It sounds pretty grim, doesn't it? I've seen this method of hiring used over and over again. On the surface, it even appears to work and can even occasionally result in a good hiring decision. Unfortunately, many times this process results in less than satisfactory candidates getting hired at the expense of well-qualified people. Everyone suffers from a bad hiring decision, but the process just described does little to help find the right person for the position. What it does do, though, is cover everyone's behind. If the hire doesn't work out, everyone involved can say they went through the motions and followed procedure.

That all sounds pretty hopeless, doesn't it? Believe me, this is a heck of a lot of work to find someone who isn't the right candidate for the position. The worst part about it—from a manager's point of view—is it can be difficult to fire someone once they have been hired and are beyond the typical 90-day probationary period.

Even worse, hiring the wrong person puts stress on that person. She got very excited about the new position, left her old job, maybe even moved across the country, told all of her friends, and started to build up relationships in the new workplace. She did all this only to find out—and it is usually a complete shock—that she isn't the right person for the job.

This whole process is not fair to anyone involved. Those who get rejected because they didn't have the perfect resume don't get the opportunity to to at least be considered for the position. The people who are hired because they have a good resume or interview well but are not qualified cause harm in the form of lost opportunities, reduced profits and discouragement to the rest of the staff.

There has to be a better way. Luckily, there is a much better method of finding and hiring people; unfortunately, it's generally not taught in any schools and not covered in very many classes.

The answer is networking.

The most successful way to hire quality people is to reach out to your network of contacts. If you've done a reasonable job at maintaining those contacts and staying up-to-date, you might be surprised what you get back.

Networking

By networking, I mean getting out there in both the real and online worlds and talking with people and groups, creating connections, staying in communication, and building relationships.

The answer to the problem of finding quality people for a position that fits within your business culture is using the connections that you build up and maintain over time.

The downside of networking is it's not something you can do in a matter of a day, week, or even a month. You have to be networking every single day, all of the time.

For those of us who are a little more introverted than others, networking can be a real challenge. That's because it requires actually talking to people, building relationships, and getting out into the world. Sure, the Internet can be useful for connecting with people, and especially useful for maintaining communications over long distances, but nothing beats talking with someone face-to-face.

So how do you network? You make contacts with people on a regular basis and remain connected with them as time goes on. Those can come from conventions, classes, vacations, or any number of other places where you run into people who have similar interests, backgrounds, philosophies, or anything else relevant.

Connections can also come from sites such as LinkedIn®, which is an excellent place to meet like-minded professionals

Networking

on the Internet. These professional social networking sites are even more valuable for remaining in contact over time.

LinkedIn is the best professional social networking site in the world today. It is useful for making connections and staying in touch with people that I know in the professional world. I highly recommend that you create a very professional LinkedIn profile, update it regularly and use it as a regular part of your daily routine. There are, of course, other social networking sites, but none of them is as useful as LinkedIn for professionals.

To be successful at networking, it needs to become a part of your standard daily routine. To keep your relationships fresh, reach out in some manner occasionally to let them know what's going on with you. More importantly, ask if there's any way you can be of assistance to them.

This doesn't mean you have to send an email out to everybody you know all the time. There are many ways that you can network that don't involve individual emails.

LinkedIn allows you to post articles that will be seen by everybody connected with or following you. This is an excellent way to keep these connections up-to-date on how you're doing in your profession, the knowledge you've gained, and other useful knowledge that you want to pass on. This updates all of your connections at the same time and builds up a rapport with people that you know.

You can create a blog and regularly post articles containing information that is of interest to your connections. The articles don't have to be lengthy, and the blog doesn't need to be complicated. Using WordPress, you can set one up in a matter of a few hours, or, of course, you can hire someone to do it for you.

Strategies such as these are passive methods to enhance your networking, but there is another step that brings it to a new level.

Part of your daily routine should consist of being of assistance to other members of your network. In other words, if someone is out, occasionally respond and be as helpful as possible (assuming, of course, that there is some way you can help the person.)

For example, if I needed a ghostwriter, I'd reach out to some of my friends on LinkedIn, plus those in my address book, and make it known. Odds are, I would get a few responses back of quality people who can perform ghostwriting tasks.

If there were a position open within my company, I would reach out to my connections on LinkedIn and in the real world, letting them know what kind of person I needed for that job. Since I've been in communication with them already, that forms a bond—not necessarily friendship, but at least some affinity. Also, if I went beyond that and actually offered actually to help them on some small task, they may be even more likely to want to return the favor.

Thus, when you reach out and ask for help, say a position that needs to be filled, you are likely to get back a response or two. The advantage of this is that these people are recommended by someone you trust. That's what makes networking far superior to blindly looking for people through agencies, advertising, and other traditional methods.

Generally, someone you trust is going to recommend a quality solution to your problem. People tend to endorse quality solutions; this enhances their reputation, makes them feel good, and helps someone they know. Most people like to help their friends and try to avoid causing them harm. Thus, getting a recommendation from one of your connections means the individual who gave it has most likely had a good experience.

Keeping your network up-to-date doesn't have to take lots of your time – just add it to your daily routine. Every day I create one short post for LinkedIn, generally about 3 to 5 paragraphs long and often about something that I learned recently. Then I create three or four recommendations for people that I'm connected with on LinkedIn, and ask for a recommendation or two from others. After that, I go over to one of my blogs—I have four of them—and create a longer article. When I'm done with that, I post a link to all of my social media accounts. Next I take a quick look through what's happening on LinkedIn®, Google+®, and Facebook®, and comment on a few posts. During this process, I may send out a few emails or messages on LinkedIn or one of the other social networks.

That whole process generally requires about an hour to an hour and a half each day. That might seem like a lot of time, except I don't watch television; instead, I maintain my social network.

Throughout the day, I make it a point to answer emails as soon as possible after I receive them. If I don't have the information needed to answer them right away, I at least acknowledge receiving the message.

I receive quite a few newsletters, and most of them have links to blogs or forums. As I read these newsletters, I make it a point to comment on the blogs or forums in some helpful manner.

I'd say the total time I spend social networking each day is generally less than two hours. Because these tasks are sprinkled throughout my entire day, they don't tend to be burdensome.

Let's go over some of that in a little more detail.

First, assuming you have a LinkedIn account, create a post now and then, on a daily or at least weekly basis, about something you feel will be of interest to your connections. This doesn't have to be lengthy; a few paragraphs will do just fine. You might link to an article that may be of benefit to others. You could relay some humorous story of something that happened to you or that you observed. You might share what you learned in a class that you are attending. Your connections will get used to these updates and will begin to see you as an influencer and valuable.

If you have a blog, do the same thing. Write a short article occasionally, once or twice a week, filling in those who read your blog about something that is of interest. Your blog might be a little more personal than your LinkedIn; it might be about gardening or golf, or something else you're passionate about. This helps create credibility with your connections by adding a bit of humanity to the mix.

Networking

As you're looking through the newsfeeds on your LinkedIn and other forums, make brief updates that assist others who ask for help or information as appropriate. Keep your responses short, to the point, and noncontroversial. The idea is to give a little help to your connections, not to start debates and waste a lot of time.

And, of course, if you receive any messages that are addressed to you, take the time to answer them. Your response will be appreciated even if it's only a brief sentence or two. Give what help you can.

In the real world, attend networking groups occasionally, go to conventions now and then, and attend training when you can. As you do these things, connect with people, talk to them, find out about them, and see if you can help them or if they can help you. Of course, get their contact information and connect with them on LinkedIn.

I generally like to spend about one to two hours a day networking. I do this instead of reading the news, updating Facebook, playing on my smartphone, or doing any other mindless tasks that people tend to do. Networking is far more valuable and a lot more fun than those other activities. The long-range benefits can be phenomenal.

How does that fit into hiring? When you need to hire someone, get the word out on your network. Call people you know on the phone or send them emails, make a note on your blog or in your LinkedIn status that you need someone or talk to people at local networking events.

Those people that I've employed due to recommendations from others in my network virtually always work out. In contrast, those that I've hired using the standard method of sorting through resumes and calling job shops tend to be lower quality performers who don't last very long.

In today's world, I've learned through hard experience that building and maintaining a quality network of professionals helps me maintain a high level of success in life and in my career.

The best side effect of hiring good people is that discipline becomes very light. Productive, competent, and ethical people tend not to require much in the way of disciplining. On the other hand, those who are not competent at what they do and make no effort to fix it (by taking courses and such), are not productive.

Discipline

One evening an old Cherokee Indian told his grandson about a battle that goes on inside people. He said, 'My son, the battle is between two 'wolves' inside us all. One is Evil. It is anger, envy, jealousy, sorrow, regret, greed, arrogance, self-pity, guilt, resentment, inferiority, lies, false pride, superiority, and ego.

The other is good. It is joy, peace, love, hope, serenity, humility, kindness, benevolence, empathy, generosity, truth, compassion and faith.'

The grandson thought about it for a minute and then asked his grandfather: 'Which wolf wins?'

The old Cherokee simply replied, 'The one you feed.'

Virtually all managers focus their energies on employees who are not doing well. Think about it for a minute. The manager agonizes over employees who are screwing up, antagonizing others, or not playing as part of the team. A supervisor might spend countless hours working with a poorly performing employee to correct their behavior or improve their competence.

Stop doing that. Why in the world are you focusing on the negative?

Just knock it off. Focus on the positive. Put your energy into those people who are performing well, or are at least doing their job in a satisfactory manner. When a subordinate behaves in a way that needs to be corrected, then get it corrected. Don't agonize over it, spend a lot of time talking and documenting it, and don't put a lot of energy into it. If you focus on the negative, you may find that you get more negative coming back at you. By targetting the positive, you may very well find everyone becomes more productive.

Most of all, don't stress out about the problem employees. Just give them the choice of fixing the problem or finding another place to be. We're not talking about the person who, like every single one of us, makes a mistake here and there – this is about those who do not or cannot correct their behavior. Tell them to fix it or get lost.

This may make your life as a manager a lot easier.

When I was first promoted in a supervisory position way back in 1982, I had absolutely no training or knowledge about how to discipline people. On top of that, it was not clear to me whether it should be harsh, light, or something in between.

There were times when the boss made a critical comment to me about something I'd done. It never was a good feeling being told I was doing something wrong or that I needed to shape up. I resolved to correct the issue as best I could so I wouldn't hear about it again.

I'm using the term discipline to include any time the boss has to correct a subordinate. This could be anything from a quick comment to a formal write up filed in the human resources department.

Discipline is an attempt to correct the behavior of a subordinate.

That's all it is. As you can see from this definition, firing does not count, since there is no attempt to correct behavior. However, there is one exception: when someone has to be fired to correct the behavior of others in the department.

Note the use of the word behavior; this is vital. A person should never be disciplined for their thoughts, personal life, or opinions. Doing so creates a feeling of harassment, and in some cases it can even lead to lawsuits.

The only thing you should ever discipline someone for is their behavior. They're doing something wrong, or they did something wrong, and that is what needs to be corrected.

If the goal is to correct bad behavior, then when is the best time to discipline a subordinate?

I learned through hard experience it's best to get it over with as soon as a problem is spotted. It's never a good idea to wait; get it over with fast, get it over with now, and keep it light if you can.

I learned that the sooner incorrect behaviors are corrected, the less discipline is needed. Conversely, the longer you wait and put up with improper behavior, the harder it becomes to correct and, even worse, the more others learn from the example.

In other words, failing to correct problem behavior quickly can lead to others assuming it was okay and emulating that behavior. I've seen this happen many times over the course of my career. For example, allowing one employee to wander in late for meetings has often resulted in several employees learning that they could come late to meetings. In this case, avoiding a simple conversation on the first instance directly led to harsher conversations with several people a few months later.

Allowing improper behavior to continue can set you up for a lawsuit in the future. If you have to fire someone because they are not competent, but it took two years for you to take that action, then they could, perhaps rightfully, claim that you terminated them without good reason. After all, if they were not competent, then why wasn't it handled long before?

People generally want to do well in their job. I found that, as a rule, the people who have worked for me actually wanted to be productive, competent, and deliver quality products. There were exceptions, of course, and these had to be dealt with harshly, but the vast majority didn't require more than a few minor course corrections here and there.

Discipline should always be done in private, regardless of whether it is a simple comment or a harshly delivered reprimand and written warning.

I'm sure there have been occasions where you've been chewed out by your boss in front of your teammates or others in the company. It didn't feel right, did it? The subordinate already feels bad because he's receiving a critical comment, so why make it worse by doing it in public?

For light discipline, which should be normal, you might take your subordinate into a corner of the room or down the hall and have a quick chat. For something more serious, go into a conference room or outside, away from the building. Just don't do it in front of anyone else, because it tends to erode their authority and make them feel even worse than they're already going to feel.

I worked for a man who enjoyed taking a subordinate to lunch to deliver a reprimand. I think he felt it softened the blow, or perhaps showed the subordinate still had value even though he was getting chewed out. I felt this made the situation awkward—it just didn't feel right. A lunch is a reward of sorts, and giving a reprimand over lunch sends mixed signals. My advice is never to deliver reprimands or even light discipline along with a reward.

Incompetence is a word that has taken on a derogatory meaning, but when you think about it, everyone is incompetent in one way or another. I've had no legal training, for example, so I think it would be fair to say I would make an incompetent lawyer. I wouldn't expect a dishwasher to be a competent computer programmer.

Incompetence shouldn't be dealt with using discipline. If you find somebody doesn't know how to do something that they're supposed to do, the correct course of action is to address the incompetence. Obviously, the first thing you have to get the subordinate to do is acknowledge that there is something to fix. The negative connotation can get in the way of this, and part of your talk with the person needs to address that fact.

Discipline

I would advise against using the word incompetence, because of the negative connotation. Instead, I would coach the subordinate, gently, and suggest training, coaching, mentoring, or any number of other alternatives to correct the issue. All options must be covered at company expense, regardless of your feelings on the matter. If you're asking someone to get trained, the company should pay for it, and it should be done on company time.

If you have a subordinate who will not or cannot understand that they have an area where they are not competent, then you may have to use disciplinary action to handle the situation. I hired an administrator who, quite frankly, was grossly incompetent, as was proven by an outside audit. This man was not performing even the most simplistic tasks of the position. In spite of my efforts to offer him additional training, he refused, and eventually he was fired.

The point is, you can't tolerate incompetence in an area where the subordinate is expected to be performing. You must be careful, though, as sometimes you could ask for things from subordinates that are not part of their job description or their duties. For example, if you ask a programmer to give a speech and that's not his forte, then it's probably not right to judge him if he fails at the task.

Insubordination in one of your subordinates is something that should never be tolerated. If your teammate lashes out, raises his voice, curses, or does any number of things to show you disrespect in public, then you must discipline them as soon as possible. In this case, you may even want to do it publicly to show that such behavior is not allowed.

For example, I asked one of my subordinates to give an outside contractor access to the database for an audit. He disagreed with this, raised his voice, and yelled at me in front of the rest of the staff. I kept my cool, telling him that emotions such as that were unnecessary and repeated that he needed to give the contractor access. He screamed, literally, that I was acting like Mussolini and Hitler, and I had no right to give him orders like that.

Up until that point, the situation could've been handled with gentle disciplinary action. However, he continued yelling, and I felt there was some danger that the situation could spin further out of control. I managed to get him to calm down and ask him to wait for me in a conference room. I wrote up a written warning, and delivered it to him a few minutes later.

Sometimes you have to do what you have to do. Yelling, screaming, and violence have no place in the workplace. It should never be tolerated from any direction on the organizational chart.

Of course, that's an extreme situation, and when it happens you have to do the best you can to protect yourself, your group, and the company. Tolerating such behavior is always the wrong thing to do, regardless of the perceived importance of the person or his position in the group.

One final note about taking disciplinary actions is that you should keep proper documentation. Maintain your own files, outside of the human resources department, of all of your subordinate's successes, failures, and undesired behaviors.

Discipline

Reports should be short and to the point; I found that I could write these in five or 10 minutes at the most.

They are a record of your subordinates' performance, or rather, the highlights of how they have done over time. They can give you reminders for review time, and if necessary, they can be used at your discretion to justify termination, a raise, or promotion.

I will repeat this because it's important. Do not file these records in the human resources department, nor should you give your boss or anyone else access to them – unless you need to use them to justify an action. They will be misinterpreted and generally judged in the worst possible light by your successor, by your managers, and by the human resources personnel. I have learned this from hard experience, having been forced to fire individuals because of reports that I'd filed in human resources which were later read by others who didn't understand the context.

These records are intended for your own use as you see fit. The problem with allowing others access to them is they will tend to cherry-pick to support whatever position they're trying to take.

Make sure that each negative remark includes a resolution. For example, if one of your writers is continually making grammatical errors and you send him to a class, make sure you mention it in your write-up as well as whether or not the problem was corrected. This way, if your successor or an outside person does see the reports, they will at least see that every issue was resolved.

By keeping up with doing gentle reminders and minor disciplinary actions for undesired behavior on a regular basis, you'll find your subordinates will tend to be more productive, happier, and won't need heavier actions.

Another advantage of staying on top of handling undesired behavior, competencies, and unethical actions is that performance reviews tend to be very easy. You've already handled everything by then, so, in theory, your subordinates should receive high ratings.

Doing the Review

"If I had my way, I wouldn't do annual reviews, if I felt that everybody would be more honest about positive and negative feedback along the way. I think the annual review process is so antiquated." —Carol Bartz

Virtually every company in the United States—I can't speak for the rest of the world—goes through this strange ritual on a yearly (or sometimes quarterly) basis called the performance review.

As an employee, I can tell you from experience that the performance review is hated far and above everything else required on the job. The stress created by this monstrosity of a process is probably the cause of more illnesses than Chernobyl (I'm exaggerating, of course.)

An employee's entire future can ride on the results of a few hours work on the part of his manager or supervisor. This can cause illnesses, lower productivity, and produce vast quantities of resentment.

My manager of 12 years had a philosophy that, "No one walks on water." Thus, in his opinion, a review always, without fail, had to include negatives. He made it a point to dig up several issues to discuss on the review even those problems had been handled months before.

Additionally, our rating scale was from one to five. In my manager's opinion, no one could ever get rated a five because, as he repeated occasionally, "No one walks on water." He also felt that no one should get rated a four, or at least it should be rare because people just aren't that good, I guess. A rating of one or two meant the employee probably needed to be fired. This meant we normally had to give a rating of 2.5 to 3.9, putting everyone at more or less the same level of performance.

All of this is hogwash.

Traditionally, a review is used to justify a poor rating and a correspondingly insufficient raise, a potential firing situation, or to nitpick a few things that annoy a manager.

I'll repeat, all of this is hogwash.

It doesn't matter how many positive points you make in a review; a single negative comment will outweigh everything else you've written. The best use of the yearly review is to justify changes in salary or position and to positively reinforce subordinate's behavior, production, ethics, and contributions.

However, in my philosophy, disciplinary action does not wait for the review. Any problems that subordinates have throughout the year should be taken care of and resolved long before review time. If a situation has been resolved, then what is the purpose of mentioning it on a review? It's already been handled and is no longer a problem, for crying out loud! The only outcome from discussing them in the review is to cause the subordinate to have self-doubt and be upset.

In general, reviews should only include information that is truthful, positively reinforcing, addressing behaviors and backed up by objective statistics. Emotions and feelings have no place in a review. It doesn't matter how you feel about your subordinates; keep how you feel out of it.

There are times when you might need to bring up something negative. I know it sounds trite and cliché, but absolutely nothing should be a surprise to the employee receiving the review. Everything must have been discussed and documented in your own file before you have any right to bring them up at review time. If you haven't done this, then you are not doing your job, and it's as simple as that. And to be frank, if you're not doing your job, then perhaps it needs to be on *your* review as a negative.

The review should reinforce the things being done right. If you've done your job as a supervisor or manager throughout the year, generally there isn't much else to discuss. This doesn't mean the employee walks on water or deserves a significant raise or promotion; it just means you let the subordinate know what they are doing right.

Sometimes reviews are used to document disciplinary problems that a supervisor believes will result in a termination. This is just bad management. Waiting until review time to attempt to justify a firing decision is just stupid. I know that sounds blunt, but when a person is performing that poorly, the situation should've been confronted and handled long before review time. A manager who postpones a firing decision or a written warning to the review is not doing his or her job.

A subordinate performing poorly on the job is letting everyone down and they need to be handled immediately. Their behavior needs to be addressed, and if it won't improve or is severe enough, they need to be ushered out the door after all reasonable attempts at correction have been made.

Let's take your typical supervisor who has eight direct reports. At the end of the year, they have to write a yearly performance review for all of these people. They are due in two weeks, and the supervisor still has their regular job to do, so they are lucky if they can spend a couple of hours on each person.

Personally, I never understood how someone could be expected to summarize an entire year in a 30-minute review that took two to four hours to put together. Naturally, my managers and I did the best we could to write and give reviews with the goal of helping by pointing out things that needed to be improved, or, when necessary, documenting issues that had to be corrected.

In theory, a review is intended to be about the entire year of performance. It never works that way. Most of the attention is on the last month or two, and the only thing that stands out about the previous time are the glaring errors or mistakes. You can bet that the errors and mistakes will be documented by most managers in case they need to justify termination later.

I've been told many times that if anything comes as a surprise to an employee in a performance review, the manager wasn't doing his job. This is absolutely true.

The standard performance is intended to justify a change in salary, a change in position or title, or to support a future firing decision. Unless a termination is planned, there's always a bit of positive or negative feedback included as well. However, the employee's attention is going to be on their raise and the status of their employment.

At one company where I worked, the review process began with the employee instead of the supervisor. About four weeks before reviews, everyone started working on their own write-ups, summarizing their performance and how well they met their goals. This would then be given to the supervisor, virtually always at the last minute, who then added his comments and evaluations.

I found most employees resented this process, despised having to write a summary of their own performance, and hated having to spend time on a task that they felt was beyond worthless. Those conclusions are based on using this process for over 20 years, and from comments from several hundred different employees.

If it's true that a performance review has little to no value in addressing the performance of an employee, then what are the alternatives?

The answer is that performance is not something that you can manage a year at a time. You have to work on it all the time— every day of the week, every hour of the day.

If a supervisor is any good, they don't wait for review time to handle employees who aren't working out. Instead, when mistakes are made they need to be handled immediately, within hours or, at the most, days.

On occasions where disciplinary action is required, a good supervisor will take care of it immediately and write up the appropriate reports. For balance, any time an employee does something above normal it should also be noted and kept for future reference.

Each of these write-ups, whether favorable or not, should be discussed with the employee as soon as feasible. Let the employee comment on them as he or she feels necessary, and then file those reports in your own personal file on each of the people you manage. Do not file them in the human resources or personnel departments.

Unfortunately, human resources departments consider any negative report as a way to build up the case to fire someone, and that is not your purpose for these notes. Keep in mind that personnel files can be seen by anyone in management, generally, and may be used to justify disciplinary action or termination. This is especially true if the manager who wrote the reports is no longer there.

My advice is to never, under any circumstances, file any reports of any kind with HR or personnel on an employee unless you're trying to justify disciplinary action or termination.

Instead, write regular reports on your staff members' successes and failures, and keep those files yourself (assuming that is allowed by company policy.) This keeps those notes under your control, or of the manager who replaces you later, and away from the human resources department and others who do not understand the context.

The point is, people do make mistakes occasionally. They also have successes from time to time.

As discussed in the previous chapter, your team will run much smoother if you give them regular feedback on their successes and failures. You also find yourself handling problems with your team members more quickly, and thus either correct inappropriate or unproductive behavior or transfer or terminate the employee long before the yearly review.

Since it's highly unlikely that companies will eliminate regular performance reviews, you can use these regular reports to make writing a review a relatively simple matter. When review time comes, scan through all of the reports and see if the employee is making improvements and has a greater ratio of successes to failures.

It's important only to note those behaviors that have not been corrected on the yearly review. You shouldn't need to go over issues that are no longer a problem. That's unfair to your subordinate since they've already gone through what they needed to do to fix the problem.

Behavior and production on the job are the only things that you as a supervisor have a right to deal with your staff. You have no business discussing characteristics such as attitudes, opinions, or beliefs of the people you supervise. However, improper behavior on the job is fair game and must be addressed.

Certainly anything outside the workplace is none of your concern and should never be a topic for any kind of review. This is not a hard and fast rule, and there will be exceptions. For example, if one of your employees is committing felonies, you might need to take action against them to protect your business.

Keep in mind that for your subordinates, the review is critical. Focus as much as possible on positive reinforcement and stick to the facts. Support all statements with objective evidence, and make sure you're not using it as a crutch for failing to do your job as a manager throughout the year.

During my own yearly reviews, nothing frustrated me as much as getting comments such as "he doesn't have a grasp of..." and "he doesn't understand..." These are not facts, they are opinions and are not appropriate for a review.

The phrase "bad attitude" is particularly wrong. How can an employee fix their attitude? Look at their behavior. For example, are they arguing with other employees or interrupting during meetings? These are behaviors and can be understood and corrected.

To summarize, the yearly review should be simple and straightforward. Look at how well your subordinate met their goals and how well they performed. You should be able to deduce from these facts whether or not a raise or a promotion is appropriate. Are they achieving or not achieving their goals and objectives? Are there any problems to be corrected? If so, back them up with clearly documented and understandable facts. Avoid opinions and feelings and instinct.

Finally, keep the review short: a page is about the right length. If you've done *your* job throughout the year, that should be all you need.

Firing

Recently, I was asked if I was going to fire an employee who made a mistake that cost the company $600,000. No, I replied, I just spent $600,000 training him. Why would I want somebody to hire his experience? —Thomas John Watson Sr

A job in the modern world is not a luxury for most people. Your average person requires their job to pay the bills, feed the family, keep a roof over their head, donate to their religion, and so forth. In other words, people need to work to maintain the rest of their life.

The loss of a job can be a devastating experience for anyone. The majority of people don't have a lot of savings or resources, so suddenly becoming unemployed can put their entire life in jeopardy. It also can lead to extreme emotional distress which can last for months or even years. In some ways, losing a job can be as bad as losing a loved one.

Except in the rare circumstance of someone who is being fired for cause, such as an illegal act committed on the job, firing is the task that most managers dread the most. It's always a difficult decision – or at least it should be – to deprive someone of their job and livelihood.

Some managers don't seem to have a problem with firing people. One of those is a presidential candidate (or, hopefully, was a presidential candidate) and he actually appears to enjoy terminating people. This attitude alone ensures that he will never receive my vote. An effective manager needs to have a high amount of empathy for his teammates.

Years ago, my boss claimed that firing someone meant that you had failed as a manager. That is a load of poppycock. Sometimes it is necessary to fire people. Sometimes people need to be fired because they committed illegal acts, harass others, can't produce or are incompetent.

These things happen, and a supervisor or manager should not berate himself because an employee didn't work out. The manager does have a responsibility to help his team members succeed, but the subordinates also have a responsibility to be competent, produce, and get along with the rest of the group.

If a manager starts thinking less of himself because he has to let someone go, he will tend to keep incompetent or unproductive employees on the team far longer than appropriate.

This is a vital fact. If a team member is not holding up their end of the bargain by not producing, being incompetent in what they do, causing trouble, being dishonest, acting unethically, or by not functioning as a team member, than it is the responsibility of a manager to fix that problem.

Sometimes a little bit of training is all that's needed to correct an area of incompetence. It is important to realize that the word incompetent is not necessarily derogatory. It simply means that someone doesn't have the confidence to perform a function or task. For example, I wouldn't expect a computer technician to be competent as a lawyer or as a technical writer.

If the problem is a lack of competence, then a bit of mentoring, some training, or even a quick course can be helpful.

Team members who cause trouble, don't produce, are dishonest, or act unethically need to be handled a little more harshly. You might even have to give them an oral or written warning. This is important to start a possible process leading to termination.

The point is that it is important to attempt to handle the behavior of one of your team members quickly and precisely. If more training is needed, then get more for the person. If someone is acting unethically, then let them know that is not acceptable, and if it continues, give them a warning.

Speed is of the essence because team members learn by example. One slacker in the group can cause the whole team to slump, and if it's allowed to continue for long, the damage can become more difficult to correct.

As an analogy, you see this occasionally in the raising of children. All young people test their boundaries to see how far they can go. When I was five years old, I saw something in a toy store that I wanted, so I took it and hid it under my jacket and stole it. My father found out and made me return it to the manager of the store and apologize. You can bet that I never stole anything from a store again.

As an adult, I observed a child screaming obscenities at his mother and other people in the market. The child was not scolded, and the mom merely looked embarrassed and ignored what was happening. When others in the area mentioned the bad behavior, they were told it was none of their business. This mother didn't know how to set and enforce boundaries, and the child had learned they could do anything without fear of repercussion. Unfortunately, this kid will probably run into difficulties later in life due to bad parenting, which happens when a parent is unwilling to set and enforce appropriate boundaries.

Employees operate in the same manner. It's vital to ensure that everyone knows where the boundaries are and to handle problems quickly so they don't get out of hand.

In spite of your best efforts, though, sometimes it is necessary to fire someone.

If you determine you have to let somebody go, then by all means, do it.

One of the most frustrating situations in my career had to do with the very first person that I supervised. She was my first hire, a programmer, and within a few months it was obvious that she had a problem that was affecting her performance dramatically. She made it a habit of returning from lunch more or less drunk. This meant that she didn't actually do any work in the afternoon. It affected her performance and the performance of everyone who had to work with her.

I attempted to talk with her to resolve the issue without success. After several months, I concluded it was time to let her go. I brought that to the attention of my manager and the human resources department.

I was new at the task of supervising people, and this was my first time that I had to fire someone. I wanted to do it right. I spent a lot of time talking to my boss and human resources department to make sure that everything was well documented and that I was justified in my decision.

The Human Resources department was afraid of a lawsuit because the employee was a woman, and there was endless discussion about how to fire her "properly." The result was a disruptive, uncooperative, unethical employee continued working and receiving a paycheck for far longer than should have been tolerated.

An important takeaway was that a supervisor or manager who does not have the authority to fire someone is not really a supervisor or manager.

Another unfortunate fact I learned is that the less time spent in human resources, the better. They should be engaged as little as possible in the process, and their role should be advisory. Their job is to ensure that all of the legalities and procedures are followed appropriately, not to interfere with the duties of a manager.

When you decide to terminate someone, ensure you have all the facts. Be ready to demonstrate the reason for the termination, what you've done to help correct the situation, and prove that your attempts failed. Stick to the facts.

Your case should be so strong and well documented that any other considerations fade away. You must be able to prove that the reason the person was fired was because of their pattern of behavior, lack of productivity, incompetence, or other business reason. Do exactly the same regardless of whether the employee is within a protected class or not; to do otherwise is to be unfair to the rest.

Your case should be well-documented so there can be no successful counter-argument. The best way to think about it is to ask yourself if you would feel comfortable on the witness stand in a court of law defending what you did. If you can honestly answer yes to that question, you're doing the right thing.

Sometimes this can be quite difficult. Occasionally you may need to call in an outside expert to do an audit to support your case. I've done that successfully in the past; in one instance, the auditor found the problem was actually somebody else, which resulted in another person being fired instead.

Dealing with the Boss

"The best executive is the one who has sense enough to pick good men to do what he wants done, and self-restraint enough to keep from meddling with them while they do it." — Theodore Roosevelt

I've been managed by several people with a variety of supervisory and management skills. My best experience was when I worked directly for the CEO of a large corporation. This man understood how to delegate responsibility and authority, and he did so appropriately.

The worst was a manager who created a wall around our department and would not allow anyone to communicate outside of the department unless he was present. No decisions of any significance could be made without his approval, and no money could be spent—we had to get his signature even for items as small as a $25 book purchase. Fifteen years after he left the company, we were still suffering from the effects of what he had done to the department.

I learned many lessons from everyone I worked for, whether they were good managers or poor managers. Sometimes it is important to learn what not to do when managing people.

Presumably, your boss has hired you into a position to do a job. Sometimes that job is described in a document usually called the job description (which is usually out-of-date.) Unfortunately, that's a very rare state of affairs. Normally, positions don't have a job description at all, and if they do it's nowhere near up-to-date and what's described is not even close to what you do.

I tend to be a very responsible employee, and I like to do my job without interference. I'm well-trained, have a lot of experience, and am pretty good at what I do. Thus, I usually view interference from the boss in a negative way.

Because I tend to be very responsible, I've learned the best way to get things done is to sort tasks into two buckets: those that need approval from the boss and those that don't – if you need approval for more than 10%, then your boss is not effectively delegating authority.

On a day-to-day basis, I went ahead and performed those tasks that didn't require approval from the boss. Generally, this involved assigning them to my staff and managing them to completion.

Communicating with the boss was a whole different story. Some managers demand constant communication from their subordinates, and others just need the highlights. Sometimes it was difficult to figure out what the boss needed to know, what he wanted to know, and what he would prefer not to be bothered with.

Our business was very fast acting. Decisions needed to be made quickly to respond to changing conditions that occurred within hours and sometimes even minutes. Because every company that I worked for has run things on a thin staff, there tended to be a lot of manual effort to keep things going.

It's always been very clear that the boss must be notified of any kind of emergency situation or something that is broken. The conundrum exists regarding how quickly that notification occurs. Let's say one of the warehouses didn't receive any manufacturing orders for the day, and this was discovered at 2 AM. Does the boss need to know this right away? Can it wait until the morning, or should it at least wait until there is more information on the status of the problem? There really isn't a generic, all-in-one answer to this question; it depends on the circumstances. In the example above, I would probably call the boss on the phone within an hour of discovering the problem, because of the significant impact on the business.

This is an area where I would recommend having a good discussion with the boss. Reopen that discussion occasionally, at least on a quarterly basis.

The most frustrating situations came about after my boss retired and the new boss came on board. His needs for communication were entirely different. Although my old boss had been thoroughly happy with my methods, the new one had an entirely different style.

This is one of the things that can make the changing of the guard a bit frustrating. In my case, I had worked with the same guy for 12 years. We had a stable, well understood working relationship. The new guy had an entirely different view of that relationship, and communication was only a part of that picture.

The only way to address this is with good communication with your new boss. Sit down with that person and find out exactly what kind of communication is needed. Layout each scenario and discuss them completely. Is a status report required on a weekly basis? Do they want to be notified of an emergency after hours?

Sometimes the boss can ask for things that have nothing to do with work. Recently, one boss asked me to run over to his house and pick up his wallet because he'd left it at home. I looked at him in astonishment and asked, "Really?" I was dumbfounded; never ask a subordinate to do personal favors.

I remember a discussion with a receptionist where she complained that the boss had her performing personal tasks for him such as bringing his clothes to the cleaners, ordering and serving lunch and making personal appointments. That kind of thing might be in the job description of an executive assistant, but they certainly are not part of a receptionist's duties.

As a supervisor, you should never ask one of your subordinates to perform personal tasks for you. They will resent it, even if they go ahead and do it for you, and you will lower their productivity. If you continue to force your personal life onto them in such a way, they may even find a need to look for employment elsewhere.

There can be exceptions to this rule. On the occasion when the boss had his car in the shop, I was happy to pick him up and drop him off. To me, this is just helping out a fellow human being.

Just as annoying is the manager who changes management techniques willy-nilly. It's not that these new management techniques don't have any value, but sudden changes can be very disconcerting and wrenching to staff.

A big problem area is a manager who uses various misguided psychological tests and evaluations in their day-to-day operations. No employee should ever be required to take a psychological test, a polygraph exam, or study anything related to psychology.

Nor should any employee ever be required to have any contact of any kind with a psychiatrist or psychologist. These two pseudo-sciences have no business in the workplace.

The problem with psychological tests is they pigeonhole people into symbols and become a crutch for a manager to use instead of actually dealing with real people. In other words, psychological tests and techniques cover-up incompetence on the part of managers. People are not ink blots, they are not four letters, and they are not points on a chart divided into four compartments.

One manager used to take delight in telling people they acted that way because he felt they matched some kind of psychological profile. That manager was using an ineffective system as a crutch to cover up his lack of management skills.

Unfortunately, in today's world quite a few managers have bought into the idea that they can manage psychological profiles instead of people. Sometimes the only thing you can do is smile, grin, and bear it.

Sometimes these psychological tests, such as Myers-Briggs®, are presented with the promise that they're going to be fun. I refuse to take this kind of test, because they make the erroneous claims that (a) people don't change, and (b) people can be pigeonholed.

Handling Shifting Priorities

"The bottom line is, when people are crystal clear about the most important priorities of the organization and team they work with and prioritized their work around those top priorities, not only are they many times more productive, they discover they have the time they need to have a whole life." —Stephen Covey

Do you want to drive your staff crazy? It's easier than you think. All you have to do is change their priorities often and without warning. If you do that regularly, you'll find them getting irritable, they will produce less, and they may even start to look for new jobs.

For most of my 35-year career, the environments in which I worked were very chaotic. The priorities of the department and the company seem to change on a daily and sometimes hourly basis.

In fact, in virtually every review that I delivered over the years the number one complaint was the constantly changing priorities. I had to spend more time discussing and dealing with shifting priorities than anything else, including disappointments over raises and lack of promotion.

Some of the things that cause priorities to change uncontrollably are inadequate resources, poor planning, lack of direction, and just plain bad management.

Lack of staff to cover the goals, projects, and objectives is the root cause of a lot of problems with priorities. Sometimes it's a simple matter of declaring that everything is urgent. In fact, I remember one manager who, in desperation, created urgent-1, urgent-2, and urgent-3 priorities. The problem was that others just defined everything as urgent-1, which nullified his entire system.

In my experience, very few issues or projects are actually urgent. In fact, I've found that many of these tasks often hadn't been worked on for years due to lack of resources. To me, that clearly said that those projects were not in any way urgent; in fact, I wound up deleting all of them from the database entirely.

Not all tasks are so desperately needed, and you must resist the tendency of users to overstate priorities. Sometimes this requires some backbone, but then again, a solid spine should be part of every manager's toolbox.

There are always limitations on the number of people or other resources that are available to a project. Some companies adopt bizarre and irrational constraints on expanding staff. It is essential that additional people be hired to support the business as it grows. To do otherwise is insanity and leads to staff turnover and unhappiness.

Managers, and worse yet, clients, often set timelines for projects without consulting with the experts or going through the appropriate planning motions. In every instance where this happens, the deadlines are unrealistic and cannot be met with the available resources.

Deadlines should always be based upon standard working hours of the employees and consultants while taking into account their other responsibilities. If the deadline cannot be met with the assigned staff, then additional resources must be added to the project. It is unfair to require overtime from employees to meet unsound or poorly planned deadlines. If it is impossible to add personnel to meet the completion date, then the date needs to be adjusted.

A poor manager will take advantage of salaried employees by requiring them to work overtime. In general, salaried employees are not paid for working long hours, so managers feel they can get more bang for their buck by forcing employees to work more than they should.

I ran into a manager who felt that a standard work week for salaried employees was 60 hours long. This man was actually the number two man in a large corporation, and he stated that, in his opinion, anybody in a salaried position who worked less than 60 hours didn't deserve to be working in his company. To put it bluntly, that's pure hogwash. Salaried employees are paid for 40 hours a week of work, except in emergencies and under extreme conditions.

That doesn't mean that a salaried employee can't work over 40 hours a week – it should not be a requirement to get raises, promotions, and positive reviews.

One of the prime responsibilities of any supervisor or manager is to direct their subordinates regarding priorities and tasks. By not using proper planning or supervisory skills, priorities can shift abruptly and irrationally. This happens because subordinates are not working on the tasks that they need to focus upon to meet the goals.

Handling Shifting Priorities

Of course, emergencies happen, and they will cause priorities to shift without notice. When a disaster occurs, existing projects may be shoved to the side, dropped altogether, or moved to other teams and departments. Sometimes a real emergency can result in longer term changes in priority because the side effects may need to be handled.

Unfortunately, it's become routine for many businesses to change priorities regularly. In fact, I don't remember a single instance of the goals of anyone in any IT department to which I've been exposed remaining in place more than a month after review time. That's one of the reasons why the annual review process doesn't work for a dynamic company that's growing fast. Directions change, and everyone needs to move quickly to keep up.

Even though corporate objectives and company goals can shift, rapid changes can be very hard on the staff. As a manager, it is your job to keep change under control. You might be hit by chaos from all directions, but that's no excuse to pass that along to your subordinates. They depend on you to keep their work rational and assign goals that they can and do meet.

Keeping Your Options Open

Many people live on the edge, surviving from paycheck to paycheck with no resources to back them up for emergencies and disasters. This is not a good way to enjoy life, live to the fullest, and cause dreams to come true.

Living at the level of bare survival places an inordinate amount of importance on maintaining employment. This can lead to making decisions on the job that, strictly speaking, violate your code of ethics and integrity. In other words, the financial stress of your personal life can lead to extreme stress in your work life.

Regardless of the state of your finances, it's important that you keep your options open so that if something does happen to your employment, you have choices available to you. Without a cushion – six months of paychecks in the bank – you'll be under extreme stress if you lose your job.

A major component of networking is to maintain your options in case you need to make a move from your current employer. Keeping good contacts with others in your industry, especially those in influential or leadership positions, can be of extreme benefit if the worst happens.

The first company I worked for got very shaky financially in its third year. Thirty percent of the workforce was laid off, and the owners paid payroll off of their personal credit cards. None of this was a good sign. The handwriting was on the wall.

Keeping Your Options Open

Fortunately, I maintained contacts throughout the industry, and I was able to land not just one but two positions and successfully extracted myself from a bad scene. For the next year, I worked two jobs at the same time; one on the weekdays and one on the weekends. It was rough, and the stress was very high, but I was determined to build up some financial reserves to give myself the freedom to choose where I wanted to work.

When companies begin having financial problems, especially to the point where they are laying people off and having difficulty with payroll, the workplace becomes a stressful and difficult environment. Managers make decisions that make little if any, sense, emotions run hot, and violent arguments become normal. Having been through all of that, I decided that I wouldn't allow myself to be subjected to that kind of stress in the future.

Let's start with your business card. If you're like most of us, you carry one business card with you, and that's the one for your current job. You might want to consider printing up your own set of business cards with your own contact information, including your LinkedIn profile address, to hand out during personal networking opportunities. This allows you to network both for your company and for yourself if you wish. If you leave your current employer, all of those contacts will be connected to you personally and not your work.

Let's move on to the resume. If you're looking for a job, at some point you're going to be asked to deliver your resume. You must have one ready, and it needs to be up-to-date. But the standard resume process has some issues. Keep in mind that most managers don't use these documents to find people; instead, they use them to eliminate people based on keywords, education, industries, and so forth.

In fact, if you submit your resume to a job hunting service or website, most likely automated keyword matching software will be used to pre-eliminate you from positions.

Managers just receive too many resumes; I have received hundreds and, in some cases, thousands of resumes for a single opening. For one in particular, I filled almost a dozen boxes with rejected resumes. It was beyond ridiculous in that most of the applicants were totally unqualified; I'm not even sure they read the advertisement.

But resumes don't tell you if the applicant is qualified. These pieces of paper just list skills, experience, and education without saying anything about the person.

However, since you will be asked to provide one, be sure you update your resume at least on a yearly basis. Then if you're asked for it, it's ready to deliver.

It's more important to update your LinkedIn profile and keep it up-to-date on a regular basis. In fact, make it a point to update it, even in a small way, on a weekly basis. This keeps it fresh and in the eyes of the LinkedIn search engine. You can find out more about how to create a person brand on LinkedIn in the book Focus on LinkedIn.

Spend a lot of time on your profile. You may even want to hire an expert company such as LinkedIn Makeover to create your initial profile for you. From personal experience, LinkedIn is an essential part of job-hunting in the modern age.

LinkedIn® is a good base of operations, so to speak, for your online networking efforts. Use it to build and maintain a list of contacts of people in your network. Don't use social networking sites such as Facebook® for maintaining your business network. These other social networks are more useful for personal contacts, friends, and relatives than they are for business networking. Also, it's not wise to mix your personal and business network. Your boss or future employer don't need to know about your party experiences or daily personal activities.

The most significant action you can take to keep your options open is to network. Every time you take a class or course, make it a point to meet people, get their contact information, and connect with them on LinkedIn.

If you attend a conference, talk to every person you can, give them your business card, and connect with them on LinkedIn.

Every contact you make with anybody who's related to your profession or business should be added to your LinkedIn network. This way you can remain connected with all of these people, regardless of what happens to your employment.

Stay connected with all the people in your network. Use LinkedIn to send occasional emails, post updates, and make yourself known. You don't have to spend a lot of time on it, but you should keep the network groomed.

Additionally, pick up the phone and call some of your contacts now and then, visit them if they are local, listen to them, and offer to help if there's some way you can be of benefit. All of this can be useful for your current employer, but it's even more important for you to strengthen your network and keep it strong so it is a benefit for you if and when you leave your employer.

One of the things that I've always found flabbergasting is how little training the people that I've managed desired. Personally, I've taken over 75 courses, most directly related to my job, during my post-college work career. I make it a point always to be taking a course, and that's easy in these days of online education.

Keep your skills and your knowledge up-to-date. This makes you more valuable to your current employer and gives you more options if you suddenly need to find a new job.

Some people believe that certifications are not important. Let me tell you, from an employer's point of view, a certificate is a valuable method to demonstrate that a person is continuing their education and meets the basic standards of that area of knowledge. The important thing is not the piece of paper or the subject matter; the critical point is that the individual is making a continuing effort to remain up-to-date and get ahead of the knowledge in his field.

That says quite a bit about the person. If I have two candidates that are otherwise equal, and one of them shows that she is continuing to take classes while the other isn't, who do you think is going to get the job? Continuing education is vital to success in your profession.

Although this book is not about finances and retirement and such, make sure that you have enough resources to survive being unemployed for at least six months. This needs to be in a relatively liquid form, meaning that you can get the money when you need it. In other words, a backup plan to sell your house if you need some quick cash probably isn't a good idea, because the sale may take too long.

I'm sure you can think of other ways to keep your options open in case the worst happens, or if you decide to leave on your own.

The best advice that I can give is to spend a little time and mentally put yourself in the position that you're no longer employed. How ready are you? Do you have the finances to survive? Do you know people in your industry to talk to about consulting or possible employment? Think about it, and based on your conclusions, come up with a plan and put it into action.

It's always wise to be ready for that contingency. This will help you sleep better, will be of benefit to your family and friends, and may even make you a better employee at your current job. I found that I've always done better if I have options.

Do yourself a favor and ensure that you have your options planned so you can make the right decision when the time comes.

Conclusion

So as I said at the beginning of this book, this is not intended to give you new project management tools, job-hunting techniques, or anything of that nature. The idea here was to give you the benefit of some of the knowledge that I've gained through my own personal experience.

Your success or failure depends upon the people whom you supervise or manage. If you hire good people and provide a safe environment for them to work, then they will support you and you will prosper. Conversely, unmotivated, incompetent, or unethical people will harm your team and your business.

You have to manage your boss, as strange as that seems. Your boss is a busy person, and the more that you can manage her by guiding her to the right solution, the easier your job will become.

Firing is unpleasant, and dishing out discipline is never fun, but you must do it when needed. Hesitation isn't going to help anyone.

To avoid discipline or even terminations, the best thing to do is to manage teams tightly. Do this by always reinforcing correct behavior and discouraging incorrect behavior. Spend your time and your energy on those people who are competent and performing well.

If you can do nothing else, at least remain ethical and maintain your integrity. Remember, your integrity is the most important thing you have. If you lose it, it becomes difficult to regain.

Conclusion

Thank you for reading this book, and I hope it's been of benefit.

Before You Go

If you scroll to the last page in this eBook, you will have the opportunity to leave feedback and share the book with Before You Go. I'd be grateful if you turned to the last page and shared the book.

Also, if you have time, please leave a review. Positive reviews are incredibly useful. If you didn't like the book, please email me at rich@thewritingking.com and I'd be happy to get your input.

Interviews with Influencers Series #4

TAKE CONTROL OF
YOUR PERSONAL BRAND
ON LINKEDIN

An Interview with
Richard G Lowe Jr,
Senior Branding Expert
and Bestselling Author
of Focus on LinkedIn

Richard G Lowe Jr

Learn how to use
LinkedIn to get more
and better qualified leads

Click the link for your free eBook and
to sign up for tips

linkedin.thewritingking.com

linkedin.thewritingking.com

About the Author

https://www.linkedin.com/in/richardlowejr
Feel free to send a connection request

Follow me on Twitter: @richardlowejr

Richard Lowe has leveraged more than 35 years of experience as a Senior Computer Manager and Designer at four companies into that of a bestselling author, blogger, ghostwriter, and public speaker. He has written hundreds of articles for blogs and ghostwritten more than a dozen books and has published manuscripts about computers, the Internet, surviving disasters, management, and human rights. He is currently working on a ten-volume science fiction series – the Peacekeeper Series – to be published at the rate of three volumes per year, beginning in 2016.

Richard started in the field of Information Technology, first as the Vice President of Consulting at Software Techniques, Inc. Because he craved action, after six years he moved on to work for two companies at the same time: he was the Vice President of Consulting at Beck Computer Systems and the Senior Designer at BIF Accutel. In January 1994, Richard found a home at Trader Joe's as the Director of Technical Services and Computer Operations. He remained with that incredible company for almost 20 years before taking an early retirement to begin a new life as a professional writer. He is currently the CEO of The Writing King, a company that provides all forms of writing services, the owner of The EBay King, and a Senior Branding Expert for LinkedIn Makeover. You can find a current list of all books on his Author Page and

About the Author

take a look at his exclusive line of coloring books at The Coloring King.

Richard has a quirky sense of humor and has found that life is full of joy and wonder. As he puts it, "This little ball of rock, mud, and water we call Earth is an incredible place, with many secrets to discover. Beings fill our corner of the universe, and some are happy, and others are sad, but each has their unique story to tell."

His philosophy is to take life with a light heart, and he approaches each day as a new source of happiness. Evil is ignored, discarded, or defeated; good is helped, enriched, and fulfilled. One of his primary interests is to educate people about their human rights and assist them to learn how to be happy in life.

Richard spent many happy days hiking in national parks, crawling over boulders, and peering at Indian pictographs. He toured the Channel Islands off Santa Barbara and stared in fascination at wasps building their homes in Anza-Borrego. One of his joys is photography, and he has photographed more than 1,200 belly dancing events, as well as dozens of Renaissance fairs all over the country.

Because writing is his passion, Richard remains incredibly creative and prolific; each day he writes between 5,000 and 10,000 words, diligently using language to bring life to the world so that others may learn and be entertained.

Richard is the CEO of The Writing King, which specializes in fulfilling any writing need. You can find out more at https://www.thewritingking.com/, and emails are welcome at rich@thewritingking.com

Books by Richard G Lowe Jr.

Business Professional Series

On the Professional Code of Ethics and Business Conduct in the Workplace – Professional Ethics: 100 Tips to Improve Your Professional Life - have you ever wondered what it takes to be successful in the professional world? This book gives you some tips that will improve your job and your career.

Help! My Boss is Whacko! - How to Deal with a Hostile Work Environment - sometimes the problem is the boss. There are all kinds of managers, some competent, some incompetent, and others just plain whacked. This book will help you understand and handle those different types of managers.

Help! I've Lost My Job: Tips on What to do When You're Unexpectedly Unemployed – suddenly having to leave your job can be a harsh and emotional time in your life. Learn some of the things that you need to consider and handle if this happens to you.

Help! My Job Sucks Insider Tips on Making Your Job More Satisfying and Improving Your Career – sometimes conditions conspire to make the regular trek to a job feel like a trip through Dante's Inferno. Sometimes, these are out of our control, such as a malicious manager or incompetent colleague. On the other hand, we can take control of our lives and workplace and improve our situation. Get this book to learn what you can do when your job sucks.

Books by Richard G Lowe Jr.

How to Manage a Consulting Project: Make money, get your project done on time, and get referred again and again – I found that being a consultant is a great way to earn a living. Managing a consulting project can be a challenge. This book contains some tips to help you so you can deliver a better product or service to your customers.

How to be a Good Manager and Supervisor, and How to Delegate – Lessons Learned from the Trenches: Insider Secrets for Managers and Supervisors – I've been a manager for over thirty years I learned many things about how to get the job done and deliver quality service. The information in this book will help you manage your projects to a high level of quality.

Focus on LinkedIn – Learn how to create a LinkedIn profile and to network effectively using the #1 business social media site.

Home Computer Security Series

Safe Computing is Like Safe Sex: You have to practice it to avoid infection – Security expert and Computer Executive, Richard Lowe, presents the simple steps you can take to protect your computer, photos and information from evil doers and viruses. Using easy-to-understand examples and simple explanations, Lowe explains why hackers want your system, what they do with your information, and what you can do to keep them at bay. Lowe answers the question: how to you keep yourself say in the wild west of the internet.

Disaster Preparation and Survival Series

Real World Survival Tips and Survival Guide: Preparing for and Surviving Disasters with Survival Skills – CERT (Civilian Emergency Response Team) trained and Disaster Recovery Specialist, Richard Lowe, lays out how to make you, your family, and your friends ready for any disaster, large or small. Based upon specialized training, interviews with experts and personal experience, Lowe answers the big question: what is the secret to improving the odds of survival even after a big disaster?

Creating a Bug Out Bag to Save Your Life: What you need to pack for emergency evacuations - When you are ordered to evacuate—or leave of your free will—you probably won't have a lot of time to gather your belongings and the things you'll need. You may have just a few minutes to get out of your home. The best preparation for evacuation is to create what is called a bug out bag. These are also known as go-bags, as in, "grab it and go!"

Professional Freelance Writer Series

How to Operate a Freelance Writing Business, and How to be a Ghostwriter – Proven Tips and Tricks Every Author Needs to Know about Freelance Writing: Insider Secrets from a Professional Ghostwriter – This book explains how to be a ghostwriter, and gives tips on everything from finding customers to creating a statement of work to delivering your final product.

How to Write a Blog That Sells and How to Make Money From Blogging: Insider Secrets from a Professional Blogger:

Books by Richard G Lowe Jr.

Proven Tips and Tricks Every Blogger Needs to Know to Make Money – There is an art to writing an article that prompts the reader to make a decision to do something. That's the narrow focus of this book. You will learn how to create an article that gets a reader interested, entices them, informs them, and causes them to make a decision when they reach the end.

Other Books by Richard Lowe Jr

How to Be Friends with Women: How to Surround Yourself with Beautiful Women without Being Sleazy – I am a photographer and frequently find myself surrounded by some of the most beautiful women in the world. This book explains how men can attract women and keep them as friends, which can often lead to real, fulfilling relationships.

How to Throw Parties like a Professional: Tips to Help You Succeed with Putting on a Party Event – Many of us have put on parties, and I know it can be a daunting and confusing experience. In this book, I share what I learned from hosting small house parties to shows and events.

Additional Resources

Is your career important to you? Find out how to move your career in any direction you desire, improve your long-term livelihood, and be prepared for any eventuality. Visit the page below to sign up to receive valuable tips via email, and to get a free eBook about how to optimize your LinkedIn profile.

http://list.thewritingking.com/

I've written and published many books on a variety of subjects. They are all listed on the following page.

https://www.thewritingking.com/books/

On that site, I also publish articles about business, writing, and other subjects. You can visit by clicking the following link:

https://www.thewritingking.com

To find out more about me or my photography, you can visit these sites:

Personal website: https://www.richardlowe.com
Photography: http://www.richardlowejr.com
LinkedIn Profile: https://www.linkedin.com/in/richardlowejr
Twitter: https://twitter.com/richardlowejr

If you have any comments about this book, feel free to email me at rich@thewritingking.com

Premium Writing Services

Do you have a story that needs to be told? Have you been trying to write a book for ages but never can seem to find the time to get it done? Do you want to brand your business, but don't know how to get started?

The Writing King has the answer. We can help you with any of your writing needs.

Ghostwriting. We can write your book, which entails interviewing you to get your story, writing the book and then working with you to revise it until complete. To discuss your book, contact The Writing King today.

Website Copy. Many businesses include the text on their sites as an afterthought, and that can result in lost sales and leads. Hire The Writing King to review your site and recommend changes to the text which will help communicate your message and improve your sales.

Blogging. Build engagement with your customers by hiring us to write a weekly or semi-weekly article for your blog, LinkedIn or other social media. Contact The Writing King today to discuss your blogging needs.

LinkedIn. LinkedIn is of the most important vehicles for finding new business, and a professionally written profile works to pulling in those leads. Write or update your profile today.

Technical Writing. We have broad experience in the computer, warehousing and retail industries, and have

Premium Writing Services

written hundreds of technical documents. Contact The Writing King today to find out how we can help you with your technical writing project.

The Writing King has the skills and knowledge to help you with any of your writing needs. Call us today to discuss how we can help you.

www.ingramcontent.com/pod-product-compliance
Lightning Source LLC
Chambersburg PA
CBHW071503210326
41597CB00018B/2670